Have It Your Way, Charlie Brown

Selected Cartoons from SUNDAY'S FUN DAY, CHARLIE BROWN, Vol. 2

Charles M. Schulz

D1081057

CORONET BOOKS
Hodder Fawcett Ltd., London

Copyright © 1962, 1963, 1964, 1965
by United Feature Syndicate
First published by Fawcett Publications Inc.,
New York, 1971
Coronet edition 1972

Printed and bound in Great Britain for
Coronet Books,
Hodder Fawcett Ltd,
St. Paul's House, Warwick Lane,
London, EC4P 4AH
by Hazell Watson & Viney Ltd,
Aylesbury, Bucks

ISBN 0 340 15828 X

WE PRAYED IN SCHOOL TODAY!

I FEEL OLD-FASHIONED!

WHAP!

WELL, I DID IT! I'VE COLLECTED OVER A DOZEN DIFFERENT KINDS OF LEAVES!

MY ONLY PROBLEM CAME IN SELECTING WHAT SORT OF BOOK I SHOULD PRESS THEM IN...OF COURSE, I KNEW IT HAD TO BE A LARGE VOLUME...

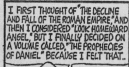
I FIRST THOUGHT OF "THE DECLINE AND FALL OF THE ROMAN EMPIRE," AND THEN I CONSIDERED "LOOK HOMEWARD ANGEL," BUT I FINALLY DECIDED ON A VOLUME CALLED, "THE PROPHECIES OF DANIEL" BECAUSE I FELT THAT..

GET OUT OF HERE!

PEOPLE REALLY AREN'T INTERESTED IN HEARING YOU TALK ABOUT YOUR HOBBY..

THE SHAPE OF THE "BIG DIPPER" CHANGES OVER THE YEARS BECAUSE OF AN UNEQUAL MOVEMENT AMONG ITS STARS...

IN ANOTHER HUNDRED THOUSAND YEARS THE "BIG DIPPER" WILL BE GONE..

>WAAH!<

YOU HAVE BEEN **CRABBY** FOR ONE THOUSAND DAYS IN A ROW! YOU HAVE JUST SET AN ALL-TIME RECORD! I **KNEW** YOU COULD DO IT!

SEE? I'VE BEEN KEEPING TRACK ON THIS CALENDAR SINCE TUESDAY, DEC. 9th 1959! REMEMBER THAT DAY?

YOU THREW AN APPLE CORE AT ME! SINCE THEN YOU HAVE GONE ONE THOUSAND DAYS WITHOUT FAILING ONCE TO BE CRABBY!

LET ME SHAKE YOUR HAND AGAIN!

I'D ALSO LIKE TO PRESENT YOU WITH THIS SPECIALLY INSCRIBED SCROLL COMMEMORATING THIS HISTORICAL EVENT...

AGAIN MAY I SAY, "CONGRATULATIONS!" YOU ARE AN INSPIRATION TO ALL THE CRABBY PEOPLE IN THIS WORLD!

ONE RARELY GETS A CHANCE TO SEE SUCH CAREFULLY PREPARED SARCASM!

HAVE YOU EVER DONE ANY SOAP CARVING?

SOAP CARVING?

YES, IT'S GREAT!

I'VE BEEN WORKING ON THIS MODEL OF AN OLD SAILING VESSEL

I WANT YOU TO SEE IT, CHARLIE BROWN...I CARVED IT ALL BY MYSELF..

I'M ESPECIALLY PROUD OF THE GOOD JOB I DID ON THE SAILS...IT TOOK ME THREE DAYS TO DO JUST THE SAILS ALONE..

IF YOU'RE GOING TO GET YOUR HANDS REALLY CLEAN, YOU'VE GOT TO WORK UP A GOOD LATHER

LOTS OF SOAP AND HOT WATER..THAT'S WHAT DOES IT!

I HAD PLANNED TO SHOW YOU AN AUTHENTIC REPLICA OF AN AMERICAN CLIPPER SHIP.. WOULD YOU SETTLE FOR A CANOE?

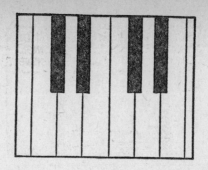

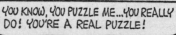

I PUT A TOOTH UNDER MY PILLOW LAST NIGHT, AND WHEN I WOKE UP THIS MORNING, I FOUND THIS MONEY...

SEE? I GOT A CHECK FOR THIRTY-FIVE CENTS!

A CHECK?!

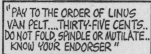

"PAY TO THE ORDER OF LINUS VAN PELT....THIRTY-FIVE CENTS.. DO NOT FOLD, SPINDLE OR MUTILATE.. KNOW YOUR ENDORSER"

EXPANDED BUSINESS REQUIRES IMPROVED METHODS..

I CAN'T DENY IT!

MY DAD CAN..

WAIT A MINUTE..DON'T SAY ANY MORE...JUST COME WITH ME.. I WANT TO SHOW YOU SOMETHING

SEE THIS? THIS IS MY DAD'S BARBER SHOP...HE WORKS IN THERE ALL DAY LONG... HE HAS TO DEAL WITH ALL SORTS OF PEOPLE...SOME OF THEM GET KIND OF CRABBY ....BUT YOU KNOW WHAT?

I CAN GO IN THERE ANYTIME, AND NO MATTER HOW BUSY HE IS, HE'LL ALWAYS STOP, AND GIVE ME A BIG SMILE...AND YOU KNOW WHY? BECAUSE HE LIKES ME, THAT'S WHY!

HAPPY FATHER'S DAY, CHARLIE BROWN..

THANK YOU..PLEASE GREET YOUR DAD FOR ME..

LOOK AT THIS BOOK...SEE HOW NICE ALL THE LETTERS ARE? I CAN'T WRITE LIKE THAT! I NEVER WILL BE ABLE TO WRITE LIKE THAT!

OF COURSE, YOU CAN'T, CHARLIE BROWN... NEITHER COULD THE PERSON WHO WROTE THIS BOOK..WHAT HE DID, YOU SEE, WAS TAKE THE BEST LETTERS AND MAKE PHOTOSTATS OF THEM

THEN, FROM THESE PHOTOSTATS HE MADE A PASTE-UP OF THE WHOLE PAGE, AND PRINTED IT TO LOOK LIKE IT WAS DONE PERFECTLY..

YOU ARE A VICTIM OF STUDIO TECHNIQUE

WHOM DO I SUE?

CLOMP!

THROW IT IN! THROW IT IN! THE RUNNER'S TRYING TO SCORE FROM THIRD!

HOW ABOUT NELLIE FOX, DICK DONOVAN, WILLIE KIRKLAND, FRANK LARY, AL KALINE, ORLANDO PENA, JERRY LUMPE, CAMILO PASCUAL, HARMON KILLEBREW, BOB TURLEY AND ALBIE PEARSON?

NO I DON'T WANT TO TRADE.. I THINK JOE SHLABOTNIK IS KIND OF CUTE..

I'LL GIVE YOU TOM CHENEY, CHUCK COTTIER, WILLIE MAYS, ORLANDO CEPEDA, MAURY WILLS, SANDY KOUFAX, FRANK ROBINSON, BOB PURKEY, BILL MAZEROSKI, HARVEY HADDIX, WARREN SPAHN, HANK AARON, TONY GONZALES, ART MAHAFFEY, ROGER CRAIG, DUKE SNIDER, DON NOTTEBART, AL SPANGLER, CURT SIMMONS, STAN MUSIAL, ERNIE BANKS AND LARRY JACKSON!

NO, I DON'T THINK SO..

FOR FIVE YEARS I'VE BEEN TRYING TO GET A JOE SHLABOTNIK! MY FAVORITE BASEBALL PLAYER, AND I CAN'T GET HIM ON A BUBBLE GUM CARD... FIVE YEARS! MY FAVORITE PLAYER...

HE'S NOT AS CUTE AS I THOUGHT HE WAS!

HEY! YOU WANT A PIECE OF CANDY?

CHOCOLATES, EH? HOW NICE...LET'S SEE NOW...I MUST MAKE SURE I DON'T GET ONE WITH COCONUT IN IT...I CAN'T STAND COCONUT...LET'S SEE NOW...HMM...

THAT ONE LOOKS LIKE A CREAM, BUT YOU NEVER KNOW...THAT ONE COULD BE A CARAMEL...THERE'S NO DIVINITY, IS THERE? THAT ONE IS PROBABLY COCONUT...

ONE FINGER WILL MEAN A FAST BALL, TWO FINGERS A CURVE AND THREE FINGERS A SLOW BALL... OKAY?

FINE

IT'S STARTING TO RAIN, CHARLIE BROWN... AREN'T WE GOING TO CALL THE GAME?

NO, WE'RE NOT GOING TO CALL THE GAME, SO YOU MIGHT AS WELL GET BACK OUT THERE IN CENTER FIELD WHERE YOU BELONG!

AND TRY TO PAY ATTENTION TO WHAT YOU'RE DOING!

THIS IS GOING TO
BE ANOTHER GREAT
SEASON!

YOU KNOW...A PRINCESS SORT OF THING...A WHITE DRESS AND NICE SLIPPERS...

AND A BIG BALLROOM!

UH, HUH...

BUT I GUESS THAT'S KIND OF SILLY ISN'T IT, CHARLIE BROWN?

NO...OH NO...NOT AT ALL..

I MEAN..WELL...WE ALL HAVE OUR LITTLE DAYDREAMS OR AMBITIONS OR WHATEVER YOU WANT TO CALL THEM..

I MEAN..THERE'S ONE I'VE HAD MYSELF FOR YEARS, BUT I'VE NEVER TOLD ANYONE..

WHAT, CHARLIE BROWN? YOU CAN TELL ME..

WHAT IN THE WORLD ARE YOU DOING?

ONE MINUTE YOU'RE IN CENTER FIELD, AND THE NEXT MINUTE YOU'RE GONE! WHAT KIND OF BALL PLAYER ARE YOU?!!

I WAS STANDING OUT THERE IN CENTER FIELD, CHARLIE BROWN, AND I WAS PAYING ATTENTION LIKE YOU ALWAYS TELL ME TO DO.

SUDDENLY, OUT OF NOWHERE, I HEARD A PIECE OF CAKE CALLING ME!

I HATE IT WHEN THE BASEBALL SEASON IS OVER

THERE'S A DREARINESS IN THE AIR THAT DEPRESSES ME...

EVERYTHING SEEMS SAD...EVEN THE OL' PITCHER'S MOUND IS COVERED WITH WEEDS...

AND I FEEL THAT AS LONG AS WE HAVE TO LIVE TOGETHER IN THE SAME FAMILY, WE SHOULD TRY TO GET ALONG...

I JUST THINK WE COULD WORK A LITTLE HARDER AT IT, THAT'S ALL...DO YOU AGREE?

YOU'RE RIGHT...TALKING TO LUCY IS LIKE TALKING TO A BRICK WALL!

HA! I SEE WHAT YOU'RE UP TO! THAT'S SUPPOSED TO BE ME, ISN'T IT? AND I'LL BET YOU'RE GOING TO KICK IT, AREN'T YOU?

YOU'RE GOING TO GET GREAT SATISFACTION OUT OF BUILDING A SNOW MAN THAT LOOKS LIKE ME JUST SO YOU CAN STAND HERE AND KICK IT!

ON THE CONTRARY! THAT WOULD BE CRUDE..

I'M JUST GOING TO STAND HERE AND WATCH IT SLOWLY MELT AWAY!

DEAR SANTA CLAUS,
HOW HAVE YOU BEEN?

Happiness is a
Christmas vacation with
no book reports to write.

PLEASE DON'T GET THE
IDEA THAT I AM WRITING
BECAUSE I WANT SOMETHING.

NOTHING COULD BE FURTHER FROM THE TRUTH. I WANT NOTHING.

IF YOU WANT TO SKIP OUR HOUSE THIS YEAR, GO RIGHT AHEAD. I WON'T BE OFFENDED. REALLY I WON'T.

SPEND YOUR TIME ELSEWHERE. DON'T BOTHER WITH ME. I REALLY MEAN IT.

WHAT IN THE WORLD KIND OF LETTER IS THIS?!!

I'M HOPING THAT HE'LL FIND MY ATTITUDE PECULIARLY REFRESHING